Dietrich Bonhoeffer

The Mystery of Easter

Edited by Manfred Weber

A Crossroad Book
The Crossroad Publishing Company
New York

1997

The Crossroad Publishing Company
370 Lexington Avenue, New York, NY 10017

Originally published as *Das Wunder der Osterbotschaft/Dietrich Bonhoeffer.*

Scripture quotations are from the New Revised Standard Version of the Bible.
Copyright © 1989 by the Division of Christian Education of the National Council
of Churches of Christ in the U.S.A. All rights reserved.

Library of Congress Catalog Card Number: 97-69106
ISBN: 0-8245-1722-9

Foreword

The cross and resurrection, suffering and the overcoming of death were central themes for Dietrich Bonhoeffer, and they permeate his biblical commentaries, meditations and letters.

In struggling with these themes he always asked for "the ultimate meaning of all life, suffering, and action." The texts presented in this book confirm that the Easter message includes the events of the Passion, the Ascension and Pentecost. The central statements of Christian teaching unfold before the reader.

To Dietrich Bonhoeffer, the mystery of this message meant the affirmation of earthly life "in the midst of the old creation" and its recognition in the new creation. For Bonhoeffer the resurrection of Christ opened up "the expanse of life" with consoling certainty: "See, I am with you always, until the end of time." From the prison of Tegel, he wrote on March 27, 1944: "So much could change, if people really believed this." The art reproductions in this book illustrate the suffering, death and resurrection of Jesus Christ and reveal how people of other times have experienced that message.

Matthew 26, 39 and 42

And going a little farther,
he threw himself
on the ground and prayed,
"My Father, if it is possible,
let this cup pass from me;
yet not what I want but what you want."

Again he went away
for the second time
and prayed
"My Father, if this cannot pass
unless I drink it,
your will be done."

Suffering

    Jesus asks the Father
if the chalice may pass,
and the Father hears the plea of the Son.
The chalice of suffering will pass by Jesus,
but *only in this way:*
that it will be drunk.
Jesus knows this
when in Gethsemane he kneels down for the second time,
that the suffering will pass by
if he suffers it.
Only through the bearing
will he overcome and conquer suffering.
His cross is his surmounting.

It is not the religious act that makes a Christian,

but the sharing in God's suffering in earthly life.

———————————

God wants the surmounting of death

through the death of Jesus Christ.

Only in the cross and resurrection of Jesus Christ

did death come under God's power,

must death serve God's ends.

Grace

We stand before Good Friday and Easter,
the days of God's overpowering deeds in history,
the deeds in which God's judgment and grace
were made visible to all the world:
Judgment, in those hours when Jesus Christ, the Lord,
hung on the cross.
Grace, in the hour when death was devoured
by victory.
No human beings acted here.
No, God alone did this.
He walked the path to the people in endless love.
He judged what is human.
And he gave grace beyond merit.

It is good to learn early on that suffering and God
are no contradiction,
but much more a necessary unity:
for me the idea that God himself suffered
was always one of the most convincing teachings
of Christianity.
I think that God is closer to suffering than to happiness,
and to find God in this manner gives peace and rest,
and a strong and courageous heart.

———————

God lets himself be pushed out of the world onto the cross;
God is impotent and weak in the world
yet specifically and only so that he is with us
and helps us.

———————

We need to immerse ourselves over and over again
for long periods of time and very quietly
into the living, speaking, acting,
suffering and dying of Jesus, so that we may recognize
what God promises and what he fulfills.

Surmounting

Easter? Our vision falls more onto the dying
than onto the death.
How we cope with dying is more important to us
than how we conquer death.
To cope with dying does not yet mean
to cope with death.
The surmounting of dying is within the reach
of human possibilities,
the surmounting of death means resurrection.

Not from the art of dying but from
the resurrection of Christ can a new, purifying wind
blow into the present world.
If a few human beings would really believe this
and would let themselves be moved by this in their earthly behavior,
much would change.
To live from resurrection—that indeed is the meaning of Easter.

This is God's new commandment, that we should look at him:

how in death he creates life,

on the cross, resurrection.

After death something new begins,

over which all powers of the world of death have no more might.

For us humans, the differences

between death and life are monstrously big.

For God, they fall into one.

Luke 24, 1–12

But on the first day of the week, at early dawn, they came to the
tomb, taking spices that they had prepared.
They found the stone rolled away from the tomb, but when they went
in, they did not find the body.
While they were perplexed about this, suddenly two men in dazzling
clothes stood beside them.
The women were terrified and bowed their faces to the ground, but
the men said to them, "Why do you look for the living among the
dead? He is not here, but has risen.
Remember how he told you, while he was still in Galilee, that the Son
of Man must be handed over to sinners, and be crucified, and on the
third day rise again."
Then they remembered his words, and returning from the tomb, they
told all this to the eleven and to all the rest.
Now it was Mary Magdalene, Joanna, Mary the mother of James,
and the other women with them who told this to the apostles.
But these words seemed to them an idle tale, and they did not
believe them.
But Peter got up and ran to the tomb; stooping and looking in,
he saw the linen cloths by themselves; then he went home,
amazed at what had happened.

The Beginning

The God of creation is
the God of resurrection.
From the very beginning the world has been under the sign of
the resurrection of Christ from the dead.
Yes, because we know about resurrection
we also know about God's creation at the beginning,
about God's creating from nothing.
The dead Jesus Christ of Good Friday—
and the risen Lord of Easter Sunday—
that is creation from nothing, creation from the beginning.

The one who says yes in faith to the resurrection of Jesus Christ
cannot flee the reality of the world;
but neither can this person be totally mesmerized by the world,
for this person, in the midst of the old creation,
has recognized God's new creation.

———————

Jesus Christ, the resurrected,
means that God, out of love and omnipotence,
brings an end to death
and calls a new creation into life, bestows new life.

———————

Jesus Christ does not want humankind
to die on account of God.
One is meant to behold Him and live.
For that he died, for that
he conquered death and hell.

New Life

   The mystery of the resurrection of Christ
lifts the idolization of death, present among us,
off its hinges.
Where death is last, there fear
joins with defiance.
Where death is last, there earthly life is
all or nothing.
The vying for earthly eternities then belongs
with a foolish playing at life,
a frantic affirmation of life,
an indifferent contempt for life.
Nothing reveals the idolization of life more clearly
than when an era claims to be building for eternity
and yet life itself has no value,
than when great words are spoken about a new humankind,
a new world,
a new society that should come to be,
and yet this newness
consists only in the extinction of existing life.
The radicality of Yes and No
to earthly life reveals that only death counts.
Grabbing all or throwing all away,
that is the attitude of the one believing fanatically in death.

But where it is recognized that the power of death is broken,
where the mystery of the resurrection and of the new life
shines into the midst of the world of death,
there one does not ask eternities from life,
there one takes from life what life can offer—
not everything or nothing, but good and evil,
important and unimportant, joy and pain;
there one does not frantically hold on to life,
nor does one throw it foolishly away;
there one is content with measured time
and does not attribute eternity to earthly things;
there one leaves to death the limited right it still has.
The new human being and the new world
one then expects only from beyond death,
from the power that surmounted death.

God's love for humans is called the cross and imitation,

but precisely therein is life and resurrection.

In Jesus Christ we believe the God who has become human,

crucified and resurrected.

In the incarnation, we recognize

God's love for his creation;

in the crucifixion, God's judgment over all flesh;

in the resurrection,

God's will for a new world.

What Does Resurrection Mean?

Since childhood when we were filled with the joy of the coming spring, with all the happiness that the warm sun infuses into our hearts, Easter has become to each of us a feast that has grown close to our hearts, on which we hang many a fond memory from which we do not want to separate. Who of us would want to be poorer by even just one spring?

What does resurrection stand for and what can it mean to us? These are the old Easter questions, upon which, in wrestling with them, we cannot fail to act thoughtlessly. The overpowering fact of the ever-renewing spring has let humankind around the world ponder an original battle between darkness and light, in which after hard wrestling, light carries away victory—the dark winter has become spring; each year the tremendous drama of nature renews itself and awakens in humanity an intuition of the hope for resurrection; all dark finally has to become light. This is a law of nature; yes, the dark is not really a being to itself, it only exists in that the light is not present—a ray of light will destroy it. And the sun comes, it comes certainly and with it the resurrection of nature. In the death of nature already lie the seeds of life.

Death is not really death, but an epoch of life that exists seminally in apparently petrified bodies. Life and light must win and death and darkness are only their manifestations. Such thoughts have been the common wisdom and traditional wisdom of humankind since its most primitive spiritual life, and to such thoughts our modernized Easter faith retreats without even realizing that Christianity has very different things to say. Not about a battle of dark and light that finally brings victory to life because the dark is really nothing, because death is already life; not about a fight between winter and spring, between ice and sun—Easter is about the struggle of guilty humanity against divine love—better: of divine love against guilty humanity, a fight in which God seems to be defeated on Good Friday and in which he indeed by being defeated triumphs—on Easter.

The End

   Good Friday
is not the dark that must unconditionally give way to light.
It is not hibernation
that carries and nourishes the seeds of life;
it is the day when the God-become-human,
the Love-become-person, is killed by humans
who want to become gods;
when the Holy One of God, i.e. God himself, dies—
really dies—by his own will
and yet by the sin of humankind—
without a seed of life staying in him,
so that his death would simulate sleep.
Good Friday is not like winter
—a state of transition—no, it really is the end,
the end of guilty humanity and the last judgment,
which it spoke over itself.
And here one thing alone can help,
God's act of power out of his eternity
among humanity.

Death of Death

Not about immortality does Easter speak
but of resurrection,
resurrection from the death that really is death
with all its terrors and monstrosities,
a death of the body and the soul, of the whole human being,
by virtue of God's act of power.
That is the Easter message.
Not of divine seeds within the human being,
who like nature repeatedly celebrates resurrection,
but of the sin of the human being and of death,
but also of God's love and of the death of death
does Easter speak, of God's eternal act of power.

Hope for Resurrection

The Christian hope for resurrection
differs from mythological hope
in that it refers humans in a totally new
and even more intense way than in the Old Testament
to their life on earth.
The Christian does not, like believers of the myths of redemption
have a final excuse from earthly tasks and difficulties
into eternity,
but must completely consume the earthly life like Christ,
"My God, why have you forsaken me?"—
and only by doing so
is the crucified and resurrected with him
and is he with Christ crucified and resurrected.

Christian life means being human

by virtue of the incarnation,

means being judged and granted mercy by virtue of the cross,

means to live a new life by virtue of the resurrection.

One is not without the other.

———————

Christ did not come into the world

that we might understand him,

but that we might cling to him,

that we might simply let ourselves be swept away by him

into the immense event of the resurrection.

The Empty Tomb

The meaning of the *Easter* message is: God is death's death, God lives, and also Christ lives, death could not hold him against the superior power of God. God spoke a word of power over death, destroyed it, resurrected Jesus Christ. What does this mean? How can it be understood? A whole host of questions awakens in us: What about the resurrection of the body? What about the empty tomb? What about the appearances?

Certainly we assume the grave was empty. But only one thing is important: God has declared himself to Christ and has touched him with his eternal life. Now Christ lives because God lives and because God's love lives. That is enough for us. We can brood over the "how." We cannot change the "that."

But if God lives, then so too love lives, in spite of the cross—then we don't live in sin, then God has indeed forgiven us. He has declared himself to Jesus, but Jesus has declared himself to us. If Jesus lives then our faith gains new meaning. Then we are the most blessed of human beings. A Yes of God to guilty humanity, a new meaning for all our doing—that is Easter.

Not being deserted by God—but being full of God, not humans and their titanic victory over godhood, but God and his mighty victory over humankind, over death and sin and indignation—that is Easter.

Death is hell and night and coldness,

when our faith does not transform it.

But that is precisely the wonder,

that we can transform death.

When we think

we can no longer walk the path with God

because it is too difficult,

there God's closeness, God's faithfulness, God's strength

becomes consolation and help, there only do we really

recognize God and the meaning of our Christian life.

The God Who Is Near

Our Bible tells us the fall of man was a turning point in history. Humans were expelled from the garden where they could live with God and now they lived separate from God in sin and unhappiness that piled up from generation to generation. The fissure between God and humanity became deeper and deeper; humanity sank into the night. And as far as humans can remember, they know only to speak of the time of the night, the time when God no longer walked among humans, and many a longing look peers back into prehistoric times of fairytales, to paradise, like to a forlorn home that in fact was never known by us. Or men of powerful hope talk and have talked of coming days, when God once more will want to dwell among human beings, when the reign of God will be built on earth. Somehow God and human beings belong together, God will return and be a guest among human beings.

There was a day in the history of humanity when this hope had to be radically ruined, when one had to become conscious of the eternal distance between the human being and God—this was the day when humanity raised its hand against God who wanted to live among them and nailed Jesus Christ to the cross—Good Friday. But there was also a day of the divine answer to human action, when God once again and for all eternity took his dwelling among humanity; it was the day when the extended unholy hand of humans was filled against all hope with divine mercy, as Jesus Christ rose from the dead—Easter: "See, I am with you…"—that is the Easter message, not the far but the near God, that is Easter.

The one who has found Jesus Christ on the cross

knows how wondrously God hides in this world

and how he is just there, closest,

where we believe him to be farthest.

The crucifixion of Jesus Christ is the necessary proof

that God's love

is equally near and equally far at all times.

Because God loved the whole world,

Jesus dies.

The Expanse of Our Life

I am God's claim on you, you are God's claim on me—God himself—and with this recognition our vision breaks through to the fullness of divine life in this world. Now life within the human community receives divine meaning. The community is itself a form of God's revelation. God is with us, as long as there is community. This is the deepest meaning of our being bound to social life, that through it we are bound all the closer to God. See, I will be with you always until the *end of time*. Again, the last things are spoken about. "I am the first and the last," "Jesus Christ yesterday, today, and tomorrow." Jesus is the Lord of times, he is with his people always, even when it is hard, and he will stay with us, this is our consolation. Should affliction and fear overcome us, Jesus is with us and guides into God's eternal kingdom. Jesus Christ is the expanse of our life, Jesus Christ is the center of our community, Jesus Christ is with us until the end of the world. For that, we thank Easter.

The Miracle

When it was evening on that day, the first day of the week,
and the doors of the house where the disciples met were locked
for fear of the Jews,
Jesus came and stood among them and said,
"Peace be with you."
After he said this, he showed them his hands and his side.
Then the disciples rejoiced when they saw the Lord.
John 20, 19-20

In the morning the miracle had happened. In the evening, the
disciples are together, and when with dawning night the shadows of
agitation want to pour over the disciples, when the doors are carefully
locked in order to be safe from the agitated religious leaders—though
without thinking that the doors would thereby be locked for the Lord—
"Jesus came and stood among them." Strange, that again and again,
precisely in the hour we most ardently hope for Jesus' presence, we
lock the door to him in fear of many other things. But far more
wonderful, that Jesus does not let himself be hindered by those locked
doors. The resurrected one does not let himself be held up by
humanity on his way to humanity. His new body no longer hinders
and restricts him, like our body does; Jesus' body has now become
the perfect tool of his spirit.

Peace

The resurrected one steps into the midst of his fearful disciples. He says: *"Peace with you."* Certainly, this was the common greeting at the time, and a good greeting at that, because it contains all that human beings can wish for each other within a greeting. But even with us it makes a difference who is speaking the greeting. The pious greeting of a mother, of a Christian grown old, has a different weight than one who just uses a formula. "Peace with you"—one would better add "is" instead of "be"—from the mouth of the resurrected one—that means: the end of all your fear, the end of the reign of sin and death over you, you are now at peace with God, with the people, and therefore with yourselves. So he speaks, who himself has achieved this peace for us, and as a visible sign of the battle conquered and the victory won, he shows his pierced hands and his wounded side. "Peace with you"—that means: He, who himself is this peace, Jesus Christ, the crucified and resurrected, is with you. The word and sign of the living Lord bring the disciples joy. Community with the Lord, after anxious, dark days, has been found again.

God's Yes and God's No to history,

as resounds

from the incarnation and crucifixion of Jesus Christ,

brings an endless, not-to-be-abolished tension

into each historic moment.

History does not become

the passing carrier of eternal values,

but becomes through the living and dying of Jesus Christ

temporary indeed.

———————

The time between Easter and Ascension

I have long loved.

It is about a great tension as well.

How should humans sustain earthly tensions,

if they don't know about

the tension between heaven and earth?

Joy of Ascension

    Jesus Christ, become human for the good of humans
in the manger of Bethlehem—rejoice, O Christianity!
Jesus Christ, become companion to the sinner
in the midst of tax collectors and whores—rejoice, O Christianity!
Jesus Christ, judged for the good
of those being judged on the cross of Golgatha
—rejoice, O Christianity!
Jesus Christ, resurrected to life for the good of all of us—
rejoice, O Christianity!
Jesus Christ—for the good of his community
returned home from this earth into his heavenly kingdom—
rejoice, O Christianity!
Jesus Christ, come from God and going to God—
that is not a new world of problems,
of questions and answers;
that is not a new moral law;
that is not a new burden to the burdens
that humans have to carry.
It means really and before all:
Joy of God, ignited in the world;
Joy of God in the midst of a people starving for joy.

The Ascension of Christ stands under a double sign.
It is the parting from his disciples,
from the world he loved.
It was a long, difficult way,
that they had walked together.
He had told them many things—but now the hour has come
when he must leave them alone.
Now they must go,
without being always able to look upon him.
Now the end of his time on earth has come.
They walk a last bit of way together—
then the last moment arrives.
He puts his hands on them in blessing,
and then he is taken from their sight. They are alone.
The curtain has fallen.
He went from the wicked world
to the heavenly Father.
Lord, have mercy on us.
Rejoice, O Christianity! He has returned home to the Father.
He prepares the lodging for you, the home in his kingdom.
He will take you home in his time.
Wait calmly and rejoice! He will return.

Joy of ascension—

one needs to have become very quiet inside,

to hear the soft sound of this word at all.

Joy lives in quietness and in incomprehensibility.

Indeed, comprehensible this joy is not.

But the comprehensible never brings joy.

It is the incomprehensible and yet the true,

the real, the alive that ignites joy.

Therefore, real joy is always something incomprehensible,

for others, as well as for the one

who experiences it.

Acts of the Apostles 2, 1–4

When the day of Pentecost had come,
they were all together in one place.
And suddenly from heaven there came a sound
like the rush of a violent wind,
and it filled the entire house where they were sitting.
Divided tongues, as of fire, appeared among them,
and a tongue rested on each of them.
All of them were filled with the Holy Spirit
and began to speak in other languages,
as the Spirit gave them ability.

Isaiah 57, 18
I have seen their ways, but I will heal them;
I will lead them and repay them with comfort.

Galatians 4, 6
And because you are children, God has sent the Spirit of his Son
into our hearts, crying, "Abba! Father!"

God's Ways

To heal, to guide, to console—that is God's doing on Pentecost. God looks at our ways. It is grace when he does that. He could also let us walk our ways, without looking at them. But he has looked— and he saw us wounded, lost, fearful.

Now he is about to *heal* us. He touches the wounds that the past struck, and they close. They stop hurting; they can no longer harm our soul. Memories don't torment us any longer. All our pains sink into nothing, into oblivion, like in the presence of a loved one. God is nearer to us than all that has passed.

God wants to *lead* us. Not all the ways of humans are God's leading. For a long time we can walk our own paths. On those we are pawns of coincidence, whether they bring good luck or misfortune. Our own ways always lead in a circle back to ourselves. But when God leads our ways, they guide us to him. God's ways guide us to God. God leads us through happiness and unhappiness— always and only towards God. In this we recognize God's ways.

God wants to *console* us. God only consoles when there is reason enough for it; when humans do not know any more, when the meaninglessness of our life scares us. The world, as it is in reality, always scares us. But the one who is consoled sees and has more than the world, this one has life with God. Nothing is destroyed, lost, meaningless, when God consoles.

I healed, I guided, I consoled, "as I looked onto their ways." Has God not done that uncounted times in our life? Has he not guided his own, often through great need and danger?

How does God heal, how does he guide, how does he console? Only in that there is a voice within us that says, prays, calls, screams: "Beloved Father!" That is the Holy Spirit. That is Pentecost.

About the Author:

Dietrich Bonhoeffer (1906-1945)

Born as the sixth child of eight in Breslau; raised in Berlin from 1912; 1923-24, theological studies in Tübingen and, from 1924, in Berlin; doctorate in 1927. 1928-29, vicariat in Barcelona; 1930, professorship in Berlin; 1930-31, studies in New York; 1931-33, member of the faculty of theology in Berlin and pastor of students; 1933-35, pastor in London; 1935-37, education of theologians for the "Confessing Church," a Protestant group in resistance of Nazism; as an active member of the resistance group, he travels to Switzerland and Scandinavia; 1934, engagement to Maria von Wedemeyer. Imprisoned on April 5, 1943, hanged at the concentration camp of Flossenbürg on April 9, 1945.

Literary Sources:

Page 6, 20 (top): Dietrich Bonhoeffer Werke 4, Nachfolge. Hg. v. Martin Kuske u. Ilse Tödt. 1994²; Page: 83, 209.

Page 7 (top), 10 (center), 10 (bottom), 11, 27, 39 (bottom), Umschlag Page 4: Dietrich Bonhoeffer, Widerstand und Ergebung. Briefe und Aufzeichnungen aus der Haft. Hg. v. Eberhard Bethge.

1997 (KT 100); Page: 201, 191, 210, 131 f, 178 f, 134, 28.

Page 7 (bottom), 10 (top), 16 (top), 46 f: Dietrich Bonhoeffer Werke 16. Konspiration und Haft 1940-1945. Hg. v. Jørgen Glenthøj, Ulrich Kabitz u. Wolf Krötke. 1996; Page: 194, 759, 472 f, 651 f.

Page 8, 22 f, 24, 26, 30, 32 f, 35: Dietrich Bonhoeffer Werke 10. Barcelona, Berlin, Amerika, 1928-1931. Hg. v. Reinhart Stoots u. Hans Christoph von Hase. 1991; Page: 460, 462 f, 463, 464, 465, 468 f, 473.

Page 12 (top), 12 (center), 12 (bottom), 28 (bottom), 40, 42, 43: Dietrich Bonhoeffer Werke 12. Berlin 1932-1933. Hg. v. Carsten Nicolaisen u. Ernst-Albert Scharffenorth. 1997; noch ohne Seitenangabe.

Page 15: Dietrich Bonhoeffer Werke 3. Schöfung und Fall. Hg. v. Hans-Richard Reuter. 1989; Page: 33.

Page 16 (center), 18 f, 20 (bottom), 28 (top), 34 (bottom), 39 (top): Dietrich Bonhoeffer Werke 6. Ethik. Hg. v. Ilse Tödt, Heinz-Eduard Tödt, Ernst Feil u. Clifford Green. 1992; Page 150, 78 f, 148 f, 150, 243, 94.

Page 16 (bottom), 34 (top): Dietrich Bonhoeffer Werke 14, Illegale Theologenausbildung: Finkenwalde1935-1937. Hg. v. Otto Dudzus u. Jürgen Henkys, in Zusammenarbeit mit Sabine Bobert-Stützel, Dirk Schulz u. Ilse Tödt. 1996; Page: 643, 859

Page 31 (top), 31 (bottom): Dietrich Bonhoeffer Werke 13. London 1933-1935. Hg. v. Hans Goedeking, Martin Heimbucher u. Hans-Walter Schleicher. 1994; Page: 330, 350.

Page 36, 38: Dietrich Bonhoeffer Werke 15. Illegale Theologenausbildung: Sammelvikariate 1937-1940. Hg. v. Dirk Schulz. 1997; noch ohne Seitenangabe.

All the above-mentioned books have been published by the Chr. Kaiser/Gütersloher Verlagshaus. We thank the publisher for their kind permission to reprint the texts chosen.

List of Reproductions:

Page 5:   The Last Supper. Psalterium/Archiv Gerstenberg

Page 9:   Christ on the Mount of Olives. Master of the Altar at Wittingau/AKG

Page 13:   The Judas Kiss, Giotto di Bondone/bpk

Page 17:   Christ Carrying the Cross, Alvise Vivarini/AKG

Page 21:   Crucifixion. Perugino/AKG

Page 25:   The Mourning of Christ, Hugo van der Goes/AKG

Page 29:   Christ: Resurrection. Psalterium/Archive Gerstenberg

Page 37:   Emmaus. Rembrandt/Bildarchiv Foto Marburg

Page 41:   Ascension of Christ. Miniature, evangeliar of Henry the Lion/bpk

Page 45:   The Pouring of the Holy Spirit. El Greco/bpk